sex & violence

sex & violence

Kristy Bowen

Black
Lawrence
Press

Black
Lawrence
Press

www.blacklawrence.com

Executive Editor: Diane Goettel
Cover Design: Zoe Norvell
Cover Art: /slash/ #6 by Kristy Bowen
Book Design: Amy Freels

Published 2020 by Black Lawrence Press.
Printed in the United States.

i.

the inventions of the monsters

little blue dog song no. 1

Sometimes, you die of such blueness, a mere smudge of the thumb across canvas. Dive right through layers of oil with a palette knife. We are all about waiting and weariness. Something beautiful and French and therefore untouchable as a woman's breast. If I kill it, I can name it. Can kick the tiny dog again and again until he turns to smoke and blows away. My finger lingers on the window ledge in a French apartment with its French mice lingering in the traps. Their death beautiful and horrible and still undeniably French. I am waiting with a screwdriver behind the wardrobe's mirrored doors. I am waiting for the bite.

little blue dog song no. 2

You are my very favorite devil, my favorite delight. The hinge in the middle of my body that opens to a room full of forgotten phone books. The strange species that quarries and worries over classified ads and classic cars. Such spaciousness is terrifying, a thick black open of the interior. The dark spreads its tentacles along the infrastructure, sings like static of a lobby tv set. The rough weather of my spine takes up a lot of space, but I can recite nursery rhymes by memory, honey my voice to a whisper. Gust and swarm until there is nothing left but the gas station adjacent to the all-night market. The single bulb above the pump. The single leash hooked on the wall.

little blue dog song no. 3

From this vantage point, all the animals are on fire. All the women piled with armfuls of broken statues and blood on their lips. I do not know what the horsewomen say when their nerves spit and zing. The inevitable movement of their hands to their mouths cupped with water. Only, that I'm speaking in metaphor, in metaphysics. The slick tongue of a butterfly in a jar. Only that I laugh, because I could die laughing here, with singed hair and the water rising way too slow. From this vantage point, I could turn my face away from him, but there is something terrible at my elbow. It pinches my wings and sings me to sleep.

little blue dog song no. 4

The cat angel cries all night, mewling and spitting for milk. I don't have the patience for anything but this—the long, slow roll toward Bethlehem. But then again, none of us are getting out of this alive. The woman with her hive of hair. The burning giraffe. Everyone drinking tea and going on and on about art. Even the little blue dog knows the jig is up with the mountains on fire and this creeping dread. It touches everything my fingers touch, but then again my fingers touch everything. The burning landscape, the space behind the cat angel's ears. He purrs and the clouds catch fire above us.

little blue dog song no. 5

A couple more seconds, and I could disappear into this landscape. Disappear into the green and blue sky. My legs dissolving into mist, my body into architecture. No sooner have I placed myself against the horizon and gazed into the distance than the wilderness is at my heels. Beyond. Behind. Between. My hip jutting toward the west. But then who knows which way is west? Who knows which way the narrative runs, sun-quenched and obvious. The grass is greener here, lusher than I expected. My thoughts are olive colored and dusty. A couple more seconds and the shadows change, igniting the horizon and the back of my skirt.

little blue dog song no. 6

The desert is full of monsters. Full of mornings emptied of their contents—a small stone, a wash of blue. The bones inside the torso are visible only to the vultures just off screen. Just off the coast, where the loneliest women drop head into hands, the flax of their hair twisting into curls. The desert is full of landmarks—lurching gods with sand in their mouths and the strange hum of broken glass. This wreckage of animal bones, busted spoons, the rusted tools buried just deep enough to disappear forever. Here, where the desert is full of mouths. Full of desert, full of rough, rainless sky.

little blue dog song no. 7

I am planning my escape strategy for when the lights go out. What wilderness pushing at the seams of me, gibbous and full. Never mind this chalk drawing I call my inner self. The tiny bell-shaped indent beneath my sternum. I say "hello" but what I want to say is "You have too many hands, sir." One is on my throat and the other inching up my thigh. My voice is shriller than I mean it be. I once dropped an ice cube into hellfire and it came back a river. Your hourglass keeps draining on the half hour and has started catching fire from the brimstone. I say, "You're beautiful." But what I mean is, "I'm dying."

ii

dirty blonde

Why did the blonde scale the chain-link fence?

To see what was on the other side.

A blonde and a redhead walk into a bar. Walk into a forest. Walk into the war. A blonde and a redhead tie two sticks together and pretend this is a fort. Pretend this a stickup, but place your hands on your chest. Place your hands against my hands. Place your hands over your ears. A blonde and a redhead thread tiny knots through tiny needles in the middle of the afternoon. Pretend they're sisters. Pretend they're sisters to the perfect seam, stitched from the same dark blanket in a field of stars.

A blonde girl walks into a story. Walks fourteen blocks in heels. Waits on a corner for a man that never comes. Waits on a corner for a Minnesota summer. A flotilla in the middle of a lake. In her yellow dress at the top of the stairs, waits through two scotches and a series of sad advances. Falls through one floor then another and it's almost like love. Walks into a story that's almost like a romance, except for the dreams about drowning. Except for the quarters over his eyes and his empty suitcase.

A blonde opens a can of soda. Opens her fist filled with dimes. Detonates 100 different scenarios for recklessness dancing on the head of a pin. There are too many scarves in her wardrobe and too many hands on her ribs. A blonde opens her body to the river and the river opens her to her accordingly. A blonde knows how the tiny machine of the heart becomes waterlogged and wrecked even with care. With *care* the thing that breaks it.

Three blondes walk into a building.

You'd think one of them would've seen it.

Three blondes walk into a mall. Walk into a small disaster filled with plastic rhododendrons and fuchsia sweaters. Walk into the dark flicker of a movie theatre where a blonde on the screen throws a drink in a man's face then walks away. Three blondes eat popcorn 'til their lips are dry with salt. Try on jeans in a narrow booth. Three blondes know the difference between love and sex but still cling to the tiny invertebrate hope of it. The magic eight ball in their dresser where the lava lamp casts its green glow. *Yes.*   *No.*   *Ask again later.*

A blonde and a brunette wait for a train. Wait for the period at the end of the sentence at the end of a century. A blonde knows her way around a man's mouth. Knows her way around desire like the back of her hand. The palm in her field of vision only an end stop. The staccato beat of swallows following her footsteps. The brunette smokes a cigarette and talks about fate. But the blonde knows her way around the short end of a long stick. Knows when to drop the stick and run.

What does the Bermuda Triangle and blondes have in common?

They've both swallowed a lot of semen.

This blonde walks into a bar and walks into the back of a man walking into a mid-life crisis. He opens his hand and offers her a camellia. Offers her a drink. A blonde walks into her thirties like she's walking into a room with the lights all off. Arms extended and her eyes closed. Walks into the back of a man walking out on his wife and walking into a story we've all heard before. Offers her an arm on the way to the bathroom, where she walks into a panic attack, all the faucets broken and the need for water fierce as a dust storm in her throat.

Two blondes fall down a hole. Fall down an entire year. In one end and out the other. By June, the basement is filling with water and the air ducts crudding with crushed insects. Their reflections strange and complicated in every mirror. Every *here* corresponding with some unknown *there* in the universe, where the vibrato of their voices shudder and waver. The wishbone of their throats harbor tiny fish and assorted birdery. The murder composed so orderly. Their bodies placed so careful in their beds each morning. So carefully in bed each night.

Two blondes go on a roadtrip. Slipping into dingy hotel pools and fucking bartenders in back rooms. Ducking checks and humming along to the radio. Running their fingers through their hair and setting things on fire in parking lots. Courting the dark corners of taverns in towns named after women—*Laverne, Eileen, Mariah*. Two blondes know their way around the dark places. The spaces between the body and the door and the distance it takes to cross. The loss of car keys and lipsticks deep in the sofas of strange men. The open road that eats itself like a snake.

What does a blonde and a turtle have in common?

If either one of them end up on their back they are both fucked.

A blonde's neighbor's house was on fire so she called 911. Called it a total loss except for bedroom sets and boxes of dishes littering the curb out front for months. Called it karma for drunken fistfights and a poisoned cat. Called it heads when it should have been tales. Tales when it should have been heads. The blonde called her mother that night and called her a *bitch* for saying what she could have been saying all along. Called the day a total loss except for the cigarettes tucked so carefully in the back pocket of her jeans.

A blonde walks into a story and all hell breaks loose. Blondeness that is. Years and she's been dying it a dark coffee brown. Dying a little more each year, as all blondes do. Wearing glasses and fucking responsible men like bankers and accountants and insurance adjustors. And all the while the brightness reappears every 4-6 weeks like clockwork. Her girl-self flaxen and flirting with truck drivers and oil drillers on cross-country trains. Years and she's been holding the rails, holding the ropes. Hoping for better weather, the forecast predicting all's fair.

How do you keep a blonde busy all day?

Put her in a round room and tell her to sit in the corner.

A blonde writes poems about sleeping with a married man. Loves the old school suburban tawdriness of him. Key parties and the insider tradingness of him. How he tastes sometimes like cigarettes, sometimes like strawberry gum. She mouths to herself several times a day the phrase *other woman* but the words stick in the throat. But she still likes the way his hand wanders over her back appreciatively in elevators, as if she were a new car with its shininess and new car smell.

A blonde floats in a swimming pool. Floats over the shadow of her body floating over the bottom. Water radiating off her in ripples. It's all riptide and plunder, over and under. A blonde floats in a swimming pool and her lover wavers over and under her body. Floating over and under the midwestern sun. Over and under the body that shivers in the shade of his shadow.

How do you get a blonde pregnant?

Come in her shoes and let the flies do the rest.

A blonde walks into a drugstore and winces beneath the fluorescents. Pockets toothbrushes and tampax. Tucks a pregnancy test beneath her jacket. It's a racket, she thinks later, the cool porcelain of "no" assured. The probability of biology and timing blurring her vision. A blonde walks into a drugstore and lurks all night in the *feminine hygiene* aisle, imagining how many people are having sex right this minute. Divided by an endless number of eggs being released right this minute. And right this minute. And this minute. And this.

A blonde spends exactly 12 hours per year dying her hair. X hours per year in elevators staring at the space above the numbers awkwardly. X hours a year staring at her face in the mirror. Spends 300 plus hours waiting to rinse—her hair, her mouth, the dishes in the sink. 40 hours a week in the job she secretly hates, but is secretly waiting to get fired from. 20 minutes a day staring at the bathroom tiles and humming to herself. 15 minutes a day pulling herself out from under sleep and another 16 hours or so waiting to get back there.

A blonde bakes a cake in the middle of the night. Waits for the edges to brown perfectly on all four corners. In bed, watches *Hoarders*, where a woman wades knee deep through a sea of empty toilet paper rolls and soggy newspaper in a tattered fur coat. It's so domestic, so perfectionistic. Where the hem of the coat meets the flooded living room carpet. Alarming how much the blonde wants to gather everything to her—dresses and men and books with their spines broken. To feather her mattress with tiny crystal animals. Their jeweled eyes staring blankly and exquisite.

A redhead tells her blonde stepsister, "I slept with a Brazilian..."

The blonde replies, "Oh my God! You slut! How many is a

brazilian?"

A blonde works in a library, runs her fingers daily over the sad cards of the card catalog. Collects them in her purse, where nightly, she writes poems on the backside of THE COMPLETE POEMS OF EMILY DICKINSON. Pens a grocery list on NATURAL HAZARDS AND DISASTERS. Days later she finds the single word BANANA on the TROPIC OF CANCER. Why did the blonde get thrown out of the banana factory? She was throwing out all the bent ones.

A blonde walks into a story and the story crumbles. A few feathers escape from her throat, but you can't hear for all of the wind. Can't hear for all the windows blacked out in her mind. A blonde walks into the middle of a city in the middle of a country and what can the blonde do but swallow herself bit by bit until she spills?

Did you hear about the blonde coyote?

Got stuck in a trap, chewed off three legs and was still stuck.

iii.

honey machine

Your dissatisfaction, on the other hand, arrived through the mail slot

       with loving regularity

The bees are so slow I hardly know them. I love them like history. Does not my heat astound you? And my light? All by myself I am a huge camellia. How I would like to believe in tenderness. We kept picking up handfuls, loving it. I have your head on my wall. And the men, what is left of the men at the end, they solemnly bong out their names.

I have hung the cave with roses

I have taken a pill to kill the pink light. The tits on mermaids and two-legged dream girls. Taken a pill to drop the red and blue zeppelin from a terrible altitude. It's little toy wife. Waterproof, shatterproof. Her bright hair, her shoes black. Packing up the sick cats. All by myself, I am a huge camellia. What is left of the men, already full of holes.

more terrible than she ever was, red

All night I carpenter a space for the thing I am given. Spidery, unsafe.

Wind gagging my mouth with my own blown hair. I have fallen a long

way, cow heavy and floral. Made a hole in the hot day, a vacancy. Here

is my honey-machine, it will work without thinking.

Will you marry it? Stop crying. Open your hand.

Pure acetylene, hard and apart

And I said, *I do.* All by myself. All the saints blue and your head on my wall. There was nothing to do with such beautiful blank but marry it. Right, like a well done sum. All gods know is destination. I am 30. All night, I carpenter a space for the thing I am given. Utterly unasked for.

It is so small, the place I am getting to—

They are hunting the queen. Glowing and coming and going. *Is she*

dead? Is she sleeping? She is very clever, flush on flesh. All gods know is

destination—the little toy wife, the ghastly orchid. Love, I am pure

acetylene, hard and apart and white. I am the magician's girl who

does not flinch. O moon glow, o' sicko. I am so stupidly happy.

Moth breath, hung, starved

On a striped mattress in the rain, the dew makes a star. I love it like history. Wavery, indelible. The light burns blue. It is so small, the place I am getting to, gagging my mouth with my own blown hair. You confess everything. You are the one, solid, the spaces lean on. What girl ever flourished in your company?

hospital of dolls

What would the dark do without fever to eat? I am only 30, my naked

mouth red and awkward. The smell of years burning trickles and

stiffens in my hair. The moon drags, bright hair, shoe black. I call

you orphan, but orphan, you are ill. The moon is a shadow. We lie

and cry after it.

I simply cannot see where there is to get to

I have let things slip. Old bondage, boredom. No one is safe from the news of you. In any case you are always here, tremulous breath at the end of my line. I am a lantern white and blank, poor and bare and unqueenly. Things are glittering, and the fox heads, the otter heads, the heads of dead rabbits. They live on, instead of flowers.

And I said *I do. I do.*

Nevertheless. I'll carry it off. Pure acetylene, hard and apart. I break

and the mouth, it is horrible. There is nothing to do with such

beautiful blank, but kill what you can. The men, what is left trickles

and stiffens in my hair. The blood blooms clean and no black sky can

leak through.

The honey drudgers, or what girl every flourished in such company?

Homunculus, I am ill, I have taken a pill to kill a bored hoodlum in a red room, spread of hot petals. He does not smile or smoke. I am packing the babies. I am packing the sick cats. Clouds pass and disperse. You are the one, solid, the spaces lean on. Surely the sky is not that color. Surely creeps away, many snaked, with a long hiss of distress.

Sick animal

O moon glow. O' sick o. Does not my heat astound you? I have taken a pill to kill the dull angels. The heads of dead rabbits. The pallor of flying iris. My box is only temporary. There is no body in the house at all. Hung, starved, burned, hooked. The body does not come into it at all.

Like a rich pretty girl

How I would like to believe in tenderness, the light bleeding and peeling. I love it like history. What girl ever flourished, so stupidly happy? The clouds like cotton. *Stop crying. Open your hand.* My petticoats sticky with cherries and bride flowers. I simply cannot see where there is to get to.

You confess everything

to the little toy wife. I smile and smoke. How I would like to believe in
tenderness. It trickles and stiffens in my hair. You are the one, solid,
the spaces lean on. Nevertheless, the papery day is already full of
holes. Your tubes blown like a bad radio. Loving it, picking up
handfuls. My naked mouth, red and awkward.

Nevertheless—

All night, I carpenter a space for the owl heads, the fox heads, the heads of dead rabbits. I am so stupidly happy. I kill what I can, and confess everything. My naked mouth red and awkward, my black on black. I break and the mouth breaks. Burns blue and expels a freshness, a vacancy. I blow my tubes like a bad radio. Shatterproof. Proof.

iv.
/slash/

1 MAIN TITLE SEQUENCE

1 OPEN on a black screen. SUPERIMPOSE in dark red letters:

SLASH

Then we slowly: FADE IN TO: Darkness, with a small shape in the
center of the screen. As MAIN TITLES CONTINUE OVER,
CAMERA SLOWLY MOVES IN on the shape. We get closer and
closer until we see that the shape is a girl. It is a large, full head of
hair, not a monster or ghoul but the pale, neutral features of a girl
weirdly distorted by the girl. Distorted by her girlness, pink panties
and loveworn lockets. By the girlness of her sighs and pink
bedspreads fluttering in the breeze. The girl, a jack-o'-lantern on
the window sill, curtains moving in the still air. We move toward the
rear of a house, voices inside.

Then LAUGHTER. 2. CONTINUED: (CONTINUED) The POV
moves from the jack-o'-lantern down to another window and peers
inside. We see the sister sistering her hair. Sistering the silence. Into
the bedroom comes the SISTER, 18, very pretty. *We're all alone, aren't
we?* They sister again, this time with more passion. The boyfriend
begins to unbutton the sister's blouse.

The POV swings away from the window and begins to restlessly pace

back and forth, agitated, disturbed. We HEAR THE SOUNDS of

the sister and boyfriend inside the bedroom growing more sistered.

———

The sister sits at the night table, brushing her hair. Sits at the table, all her girl holes open. The mask holes, gaping, as the knife plunges again and again. As the holes open again and again. So many holes full of knife and bleeding, opening and opening. She looks down incredulously as the blood forms at her hands. She begins to scream.

What's Inside a Girl?

plastic ponies

mock oranges

rusty nails

tissue paper

tennis shoes

wet towels

birthday candles

rubber cement

strawberry shampoo

driftwood

short shorts

seaweed

curling iron

hot rods

sycamore trees

Dear Murderer—

I see you your knife and raise you a hatchet. I've been watching soap operas and I'm as clean as ivory soap. Pure as a thousand blondes in terrycloth shorts spreading their thighs just enough to see the slit that excites you. Their white light, their tight tits. In the movie theatre, I am rubbing my hand over you in the flickering dark, waiting for the final gasp and the gush. Each bloody footprint leading you to the money shot, the exquisite quiver.

30 Must See Places Before You Die

rotting basement
car trunk
river's edge
dumpster
bedroom closet
gas station bathroom
hotel room
backseat
hallway closet
laundry room
movie theatre
dressing room at the mall
rest stop
back alley
bedroom
janitor's closet
suburban garage
locker room
quarry
classroom
gravel road
car park
bar bathroom
bus station
breakroom
public park
roadside ditch
warehouse
living room
stairwell

Pitch # 1

girl becomes monster

becomes merry-go-round

becomes record player

becomes living room rug

becomes open door

becomes bathroom light

becomes roadside suicide

becomes drafty window

becomes Chevrolet

becomes optical illusion

becomes ossory

becomes sorry

becomes soft with use

Dear Murderer—

The saddest thing I ever saw in horror movie was the prom queen's dress catching fire and burning her to a crisp. Not the blood and the running and death, come three times over and fat with dark. But in the car park, you watched me throw up a box of twinkies, wipe my mouth and smile. Don't think this means you know me. I am working on holding down the universe in the pit of my stomach, but it's hard sometimes. Yesterday, the football team ran a train on me in my mother's basement. My hands flat against the floor and the universe eating me from the inside out. Believe me, I am not afraid.

What's Inside a Girl?

watch parts

witch hazel

hardware

hi-fi

fire extinguisher

fine china

charm bracelets

lace curtains

crochet hooks

tiny taxidermied mice

22 Ways to Die

bullet through the head
axe through the chest
accidental drowning
arrow through the eye
bear trap
strangling
hatchet to the head
intentional drowning
crowbar through the chest
fork in the eye
heart ripped out
head ripped off
car accident
hanging (accidental)
hanging (intentional)
caught in fire
on fire (spontaneous combustion)
broken neck
broken heart
strangulation
suffocation
disarticulation

Pitch # 2

boy meets girl

meets engine

meets heat

meets abandoned quarry

meets summer

meets crossroads

meets girl behind the gas station

meets girl behind the girl

meets girl things

meets girl meat

Dear Murderer—

I am so small here beneath this bed. Beneath this dead silence. Beneath this science book. So small you have to get down on all fours. Down on the floors and scooch around just a little to find me. Find me scooching just a little further back. Knife in my hand, pen in my hand, ready to strike. Ready to write you a love letter in my sweat and blood right here beneath this bed. Where I dream about sex but not about sex really. But more about being small enough to blend into the dust ruffle that burns black with my breath.

What's Inside a Girl?

rice cakes

math problems

pears

roadside flares

rope

weather vanes

vicodin

dinner napkins

nightlight

northern lights

night

v.

how to write a love poem in a
time of war

Say you begin with midsummer. The haze of late June and dusk. The

hush of birds lingering at the treetops above asphalt. How I am

trying to be poetic, but then, isn't all love a kind of elegy to

something about to happen. The moment before or after the falling.

Which is to say not precisely falling, but sinking slowly through

water at an agreeable rate. Or stepping off a train platform and into a

swarm of bees. Not precisely dangerous, but still fraught with

danger. Not precisely desirous, but rattling with desire.

I decide I'm going to kiss you when you say you too love *Buffy the Vampire Slayer*. I decide I'm going to fuck you when later that night, you kiss me, hard, fingers wrapped in my hair. My purse on the ground and all the air gone out of me. The question not *if?* But *when?* The issue of *where?* and *how?* You know us writers, turning everything to grist. The inner machinery ticking. I know how to write about disastrous love. But then maybe all love is disastrous in its own way. And maybe only partly true. The written and rewritten. The twisted and untwisted. Every poem I've ever written is an elegy to a moment that may or may not have happened. Every sentence and gesture teetering at the edge of the platform.

It occurs to me to write this as a confession. As an absolution. Early that first evening you say to me something along the lines of "That's enough about dead cats. After all, I am trying to seduce you." I take you to the bar I take all first dates to, and you keep referencing movies I've never seen, television shows I've never watched. I smile and twirl my straw in my jack and coke. I'm not thinking about how to write this, but then I am always thinking how to write this. I tell myself *please stop thinking about how to write this!* Maybe a more poetic me would be drinking something fancier—a sidecar or a Manhattan. Or is a Manhattan technically a sidecar? But that's enough about dead cats; I am trying to seduce you.

Because the body is made up equally of water and stardust, it's the weekend and I am trying to make a cake out of words. Out of tiny miniature farm animals and the tablecloths I never use. Am hunting the volcano to throw anything and everything into. And sometimes it works—a hiss and a sizzle and the whole thing gone up in flames. Or worse, the whole thing useless and pretty as a mechanical horse. The gears rusting in the rain. They say it gets easier with every word, with every repetition. How we fall in love with the silence before each sequence, as if the next will be entirely new.

Say you begin with a listing of every scar. Every broken bone. What the body knows as trauma or memory. Every love leaves a trace on the skeletal system. Sometimes even a tiny stress fracture. As bodies, we move through the world occasionally bumping into things that damage. When I was 8, I broke my left ring finger, slamming it in the back door. My abdomen bears a scar from a teakettle incident. My forearm, the perfect triangle of the top of an iron. This is the way I move through the world. Occasionally bumping into the edges of bartending engineers and secretly married ad salesmen. Running into walls and tripping up stairs. I do not know how to write about love without a little bit of pain. The pure panic of its return. I only once said to a man that I loved him, and a decade later, it makes the bones of my throat ache.

Another summer and the bees have gotten unruly, swarming what they can—trash cans and train cars. Light posts in the middle of downtown. It's the charm of the inexplicable, tiny wings glinting in the sun. How 20,000 of them in the UK followed a car for miles, their queen trapped inside. That same summer, across the country, a rapist goes free. The girl still rolling over in the dirt behind a dumpster, pine needles in her hair and shoved rough inside her. It's the same summer I am working out the problem of us like a knot. Another improbable, inexplicable thing. I've heard bees will work tirelessly to repair a damaged hive. Mend the seams between the wrecked and new until they are indecipherable. How they will, if prompted, repair other broken things—figurines, ice skates, Victorian doll houses. I want to think this is possible. To remake everything new eventually. The girl behind the dumpster covered in honey and rebuilding, cell by cell. How each night, I am remaking something with the thrum of a hundred thousand wings.

You are the first guy to bring me flowers and chocolate on Valentine's Day and I am embarrassed at how much I like it. I am, after all, an unromantic romantic. Forever self-conscious of the swoon and swirl. Love is forever something I am having to convince myself of. A step off, a giving in to gravity. For all I know, love is an auto-immune response, biological and chemical. It is not to be trusted. Or maybe it's the only thing we can trust. Chocolate has been known to induce similar serotonin levels, so I'm not sure if this is the heart talking or the chocolate, but for a good while I can't stop thinking about that drop. The free fall, and the thing that catches.

A couple weeks in, we play *Two Truths and a Lie*. I tell you I have a tiny mermaid tattoo somewhere under my clothes. But then, by now, you've seen everything. Two truths later, I am drunk on Jameson and static. A delicious sort of panic set in at the tip of my spine. I tell you I can do card tricks, produce a quarter from behind your ear. And it's nearly the truth, but it's a deception I can't work anymore. A rope I can't untie If the hand moves faster than the eye, than the heart, I've been stacking the odds in favor of bad weather. Of grease fires and electrical surges. The urge to fuck near strangers in the stairwell to my apartment. The truth is that I love this part. The one where I stand in water holding a live wire, waiting for something to spark.

One of the benefits of dating lots of people is that you start to catalogue and identify with accuracy. File this one under "absent mother." Another under "subtext: monsters." If the chief sign of insanity is doing the same thing over and over and expecting different results, call me crazy. Call me "bird hitting the window erratically." Call me "door that is here then gone then here again." I meet you, and I choke on feathers and the shape of an animal I cannot name. A color I imagined but never believed was real. But again I am falling too far into metaphor, fumbling awkwardly at the doorway to a house too fragile to inhabit. I feel out the dark with only my fingertips. I don't dare call it "home."

The first few weeks, my face blossoms with the most exquisite sort of damage. The rub of smooth skin and rough beard, rashing and blistering across my chin. I have to stop myself from making out with you in elevators. In movie theaters. In taxi cabs. Mostly because when I'm not, I would rather be kissing you. On our second date, we walked home from a bar and it smelled like the whole neighborhood was on fire. The stars bright and clear and not at all manufactured for the sake of art. But then again, it's hard to tell what is in my head and what is in yours. What is the collective hallucination of a hundred couples walking down north side streets in the middle of the night? What ghost of us still haunts every block between here and there? I'd like to say the moon was full, but I don't remember. Only that I kept leaning in closer and closer 'til I could feel your knee against mine at the bar. Only that it seemed an important and artful thing to remember. This, the clear sky, and everything burning down.

I am really bad at telling jokes. Mixing up punchlines and losing my train of thought. Loosening my vowels and mucking up the perfect machine. I write poems called "How to Care for Your Princess Monster" and "How to Be an Emotional Ventriloquist." But I worry that while I'm pointing at my ribs, everyone is looking at my feet. Still I dream a lot about being trapped inside an enormous wedding cake—a claustrophobic swirl of sugar and lace. House fires and horses jumping from cliffs are easy, but where is the omen in so much sweetness? What else is there to do when the man comes looking for me with a bloodied shoe and a bottle of bourbon? Except hide inside the body of a huge, feather-bellied swan? I broke my ring finger once and it was all over for me. Understand that I am only looking for the sharpest item in the room to cut the girl from the swan that is the cake that is the swan.

Sometimes I say novels ruined me the way they ruin all young, bookish girls. Slowly and tenderly rotting out the light., making room for the blood dark. Love is always terrifying, full of fevers and corsets and heavy velvet curtains. You get one sweet moment of passion, then die of consumption or childbirth. Or worse, you spend your days making polite conversations over teacakes and bassinets. Literature is a perilous place. The peril exquisite as pearl earrings stolen from the body of someone's dead, but devoted, wife. Pretty, but actually pretty terrifying.

I want to tell you I am afraid of everything. Large insects and fish. Empty swimming pools. Cars lingering in alleys. Death—my own, yours. Fear is a tote bag I carry around and keep tossing things into. I worry over 12 story hotel suicides and my bus plunging into the lake. Of all the things that can inexplicably go wrong and maybe will. One thing tumbling after another like dominoes. For months after 9/11, I dreamed every night of a city in ruins and I was the sole survivor. I moved effortlessly in my new, ruined world. I carried my tote bag completely alone, even with a broken arm.

In April, in New Orleans at the Museum of Death, the only thing that disturbed me was the smell of it—death, that is. As if by association all those thing carried a scent—letters from serial killers. Faded clippings of autoerotic suffocations. Embalming tables and funeral dolls. The crime scene photo of Nicole Brown Simpson with her head come near clean off in a California courtyard. That sort of thing is as common as breathing, as common as the lingering smell of sickness and trash on Bourbon Street. Where a man I did not know shoved his face between my breasts and I was so startled I did not move. I and my sister barely blinks at the film clip of the woman outside Chicago obliterated to a smear of red by a speeding train. The clip in judgement that proves fatal. The near miss that finally hits its mark. In the theatre, at the back of the storefront, we watch things die over and over on a loop, while Bourbon Street sweats neon and rots slowly.

In the months after the election, no one can get comfortable in their skin. This wolfish thing inside me scratches at the door each night and howls. Growls at cab drivers and racist cousins in Oklahoma. Makes friends with any window I can climb out of. Anything that can get its hooks into my hair. When I was a kid, I kept getting tangled in the blackberry bush in the yard. Scratches on my thighs, my arms, my hemline reddening with juice. Even my fingers sticky for full-on fever, that twinning under some July moon. I'd love to say I don't hate men, but sometimes it's hard. Each one before you, grooves in the same record—the ones with ex-wives and el caminos and whiskey in their voices. I'd love to say I loved them, but really, I was game for anything that could swallow me whole in one bite.

A little over a year before we meet, I get high for the first time at a party in Seattle. I can't tell if I'm feeling anything or if it's the red wine or lack of sleep, but a poet convinces me to let her read my cards. Tells me I'd be capable of great things if only I didn't hold back. I'm not sure if that means I should smoke more weed or have more sex or write more serious things, but it seems like a moment I could take a wire brush to and make it shine. No less impressive than the night you pulled me out into a thunderstorm to kiss me next to an iron fence. The atmosphere cracking and zinging. How warm your hands felt against my throat. How that night a tether broke somewhere beneath my ribs and set everything flapping in the wind.

It's summer, and on the news, men continue to do horrible things to women. I am writing poems and eating cherries 'til my lips stain. Afflicted with the kind of lonely that hollows out the lungs. Makes the body hospitable to ghosts and paper boats floating the surface of some still pond. My hand is another girl's hand. My heart is another girl's blind panic. Her father the kind with too many sons and not enough daughters. Another girl's name on my t-shirt, bloody beside the tracks. Another girl's broken clarinet in a storm drain. How all of this fills a space we did not know existed, much less that it was large enough for a drowning. And worse, that I could make a harbor here, take my slice of cake and spread out a blanket beneath it. What is, in fact, the weight of love? Heavier than a heart? Heavier than the hand? By now I should be waving goodbye. But my palm catches the wind like a sail.

Notes

The *inventions of the monsters* is based on Salvador Dali's 1937 painting of the same name.

The appropriated text in *dirty blonde* was culled from notboring.com, onelinefun.com, jokes4us.com.

honey machine is a series of centos culled from Sylvia Plath's *Ariel: The Restored Edition.*

The first segment of /slash/ is a reworking of the original movie script of John Carpenter's *Halloween.*

Acknowledgments

Pieces in this collection have been published in a number of journals, including *Hobart, Tupelo Quarterly, Sweet Tree Review, interrupture, Rag Queen Periodical, Pretty Owl Poetry,* and *Tinderbox Poetry Journal.*

Some sections appeared previously as small edition zines, chapbooks, and artist books issued through dancing girl press & studio.

Thank you to the poets who have read and commented upon this manuscript, including Cathy Shea, Devon Balwit, and Gillian Cummings, as well as my little online community of writers and publications who have supported the writing included here. Thank you also to the ever awesome Black Lawrence Press and Diane Goettel for believing in my books and giving them an amazing home.

Finally, thanks most to family and friends who have supported my writing and art endeavors, and to Jonathan Frank for allowing me to mine our relationship for writing fodder while we are still together (at least until he reads this).

A writer and book artist, Kristy Bowen is the author of a number of artist book, zine, and chapbook projects, as well as several full length collections of hybrid/poetry/ prose work, including *girl show* (Black Lawrence Press, 2014), *major characters in minor films* (Sundress Publications, 2015) and *salvage* (Black Lawrence Press, 2016). She lives in Chicago, where she runs dancing girl press & studio.